CODING
WITH
RAIN FOREST ANIMALS

BY KYLIE BURNS

Express!

BELLWETHER MEDIA • MINNEAPOLIS, MN

Express!

Imagination comes alive in Express! Transform the everyday into the fresh and new, discover ways to stir up flavor and excitement, and experiment with new ideas and materials. Express! makerspace books: where your next creative adventure begins!

This edition first published in 2024 by Bellwether Media, Inc.

No part of this publication may be reproduced in whole or in part without written permission of the publisher. For information regarding permission, write to Bellwether Media, Inc., Attention: Permissions Department, 6012 Blue Circle Drive, Minnetonka, MN 55343.

Library of Congress Cataloging-in-Publication Data

Names: Burns, Kylie, author.
Title: Coding with rain forest animals / by Kylie Burns.
Description: Minneapolis, MN : Bellwether Media, Inc., 2024. | Series: Express! Adventures in unplugged coding | Includes bibliographical references and index. | Audience: Ages 7-13 | Audience: Grades 4-6 | Summary: "Information accompanies instructions for various rain forest animal themed activities that demonstrate skills needed for coding. The text level and subject matter are intended for students in grades 3 through 8"-- Provided by publisher.
Identifiers: LCCN 2023021996 (print) | LCCN 2023021997 (ebook) | ISBN 9798886875164 (library binding) | ISBN 9798886875669 (paperback) | ISBN 9798886877045 (ebook)
Subjects: LCSH: Computer programming--Juvenile literature. | Forest animals--Juvenile literature.
Classification: LCC QA76.6115 .B874 2024 (print) | LCC QA76.6115 (ebook) | DDC 005.1--dc23/eng/20230524
LC record available at https://lccn.loc.gov/2023021996
LC ebook record available at https://lccn.loc.gov/2023021997

Editors: Sarah Eason and Christina Leaf
Illustrator: Eric Smith
Series Design: Brittany McIntosh
Graphic Designer: Paul Myerscough

Printed in the United States of America, North Mankato, MN.

TABLE OF CONTENTS _ □ X

WHAT IS UNPLUGGED CODING? _ □ X

Coding is how people **communicate** instructions to a computer in its own language. Programmers, or coders, write **commands** known as **code** to give computers instructions in a way they understand. A computer follows the instructions in the code to carry out tasks.

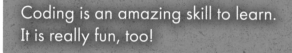

Coding is an amazing skill to learn. It is really fun, too!

Many coding skills can be learned without technology. When we explore coding without a computer, we are using unplugged coding. In this book, you will try some unplugged coding activities that will help you better understand coding. To make it even more adventurous, we will use **rain forest** animals as our theme!

LET'S START EXPLORING!

To a computer, an **algorithm** is a little like a map. It shows the computer the steps it needs to take to complete an action. The steps are written in a **sequence** that the computer can easily follow.

In this activity, we will learn about algorithms. Imagine you found a rare animal in the rain forest. You want to show a local scientist where you found it. You and a friend can take turns being the coder who makes a map to the den and the scientist who uses the map to find the animal. Try it out!

YOU WILL NEED: _ □ X

- a small toy to use as an animal
- several index cards for your algorithm steps
- a marker

LET'S GET STARTED!

Choose who will be the coder and who will be the scientist. The coder hides the animal somewhere in the yard or house.

2

The coder chooses a starting point and places a blank card on that spot.

3

The coder then takes a step, and draws an arrow on a card showing the direction.
The coder repeats this for each step required to reach the animal, taking care to keep the cards in the correct order.

4

The coder tests out the algorithm by going back to the starting point and following the cards in the correct sequence. If there are any bugs, or mistakes in the code, the coder fixes the algorithm and tests it again.

5

The coder then hands the cards to the scientist who follows them in the correct sequence to find the animal.

TURN THE PAGE TO SEE HOW YOU DID!

Did something go wrong when you tested the algorithm? Did you have to correct any **bugs**? Did the scientist find the animal? What could make the algorithm run more smoothly?

DID YOU KNOW?

There is even an algorithm for writing algorithms! Programmers begin by writing the overall ideas for the algorithm, and then they break them down into individual steps. Next, they turn the algorithm into computer code. Finally, they test it out.

HERE'S A TIP!

An algorithm should be written clearly in the fewest number of steps to get the job done. Coders input, or enter, the instructions so that the output, or action, is completed as quickly as possible.

CODING CHALLENGE!

_ □ X

Try this activity a new way. Play outside in a big space. Make up an algorithm of 10 different steps, or commands, using the arrow cards you made. Choose your starting spot. Put the cards in a random order, then follow the algorithm and see where you end up! You could also try hiding an animal, then creating the algorithm backward to lead you back to the starting place.

Debugging is an important part of the coding process. If an algorithm does not produce the correct **output**, a programmer may have to check lines and lines of code to find the bug. Unless the bug is removed and the algorithm is corrected, the program will not work.

In this activity, you must **analyze** the algorithm and debug it. You are a scientist who has traveled deep into the rain forest to study the wildlife there. A fellow scientist has made you a map of a hiking route to help you reach a group of howler monkeys and bring you safely back to base camp. However, he thinks he might have made a mistake. Find the bug in his algorithm and debug it so you can complete your research and make it back safely!

LET'S GO!

1. Begin at the base camp.
2. Travel 3 squares west.
3. Turn and travel 4 squares north.
4. Study the howler monkeys on your left as you move 3 squares east!
5. Move 1 square north.
6. Go 1 square east.
7. Go 5 squares south and finish back at base camp.

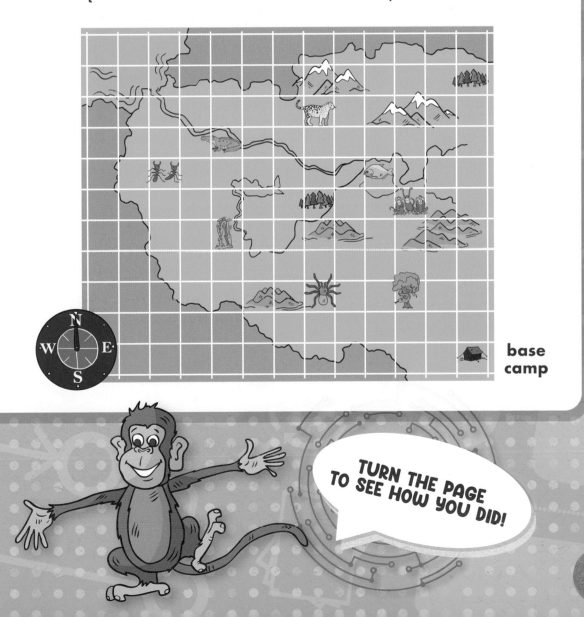

base camp

TURN THE PAGE TO SEE HOW YOU DID!

11

Were you able to find the bug in the algorithm and correct it to find your way back to base camp? Check out the bug in red and the debugged step in yellow below.

1. Begin at the base camp.
2. Travel 3 squares west.
3. Turn and travel 4 squares north.
4. Study the howler monkeys on your left as you move 3 squares east!
4. Go past the howler monkeys for 2 squares east.
5. Move 1 square north.
6. Go 1 square east.
7. Go 5 squares south and finish back at base camp.

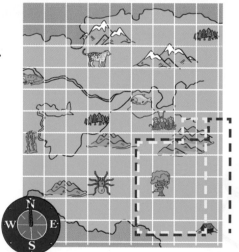

DID YOU KNOW?

Bugs belong in the rain forest, not in a computer program! The term "bug" comes from an actual moth that once caused a computer to fail!

Try saying each step in an algorithm out loud to find the bug. This practice, known as "rubber duck debugging," started when a programmer described each step in his code to a rubber duck sitting next to his computer. In doing so, the programmer heard a problem and located the bug! Many programmers use this method to find bugs today.

CODING CHALLENGE!   _ □ X

Look at the grid map on page 11 again. Start at any spot on the grid. Create a code that will take the scientist from the starting point all the way to base camp in 5 to 7 steps. Avoid any big obstacles like mountains or lakes, and try not to disturb the animals in their homes! Write your code on a piece of paper and test it out to make sure it does not have any bugs.

SNAKE EYES _ □ X

In coding, **conditionals** make a computer's work easier. A conditional is a type of command that works like a decision-making tool. If something is true, then the computer does a certain action. If something is false, the program continues in a different way, or ends. The computer is not actually making a decision, but the program is designed to include choices that affect the output.

Play this game with a friend to put conditionals into practice. Look out for snake eyes watching you in the rain forest. They belong to dangerous snakes!

LET'S PLAY!

1

Set out a 6x6 grid on the floor with index cards.

Choose one card as the start, and put your player tokens on it.

Place each toy on its own card, and write the name of that toy on the card so you remember where it was on the grid.

Take turns rolling both dice and following the conditionals. Play continues until all the toys have been removed. The player with the most toys at the end wins!

CONDITIONALS: _ □ X

If the roll totals less than 8, **then** move your player one square in any direction.

If the roll is 8 or more, **then** move three squares in any direction.

If your player token lands on a square with a toy, **then** collect the toy.

If your roll is double 1s, or snake eyes, **then** go back to the start and return the toys you have collected to where they were at the start of the game!

DID YOU KNOW?

Conditionals are usually written as if/then statements. Coders can also include an else statement to add more command options to the code. For example, **if** the sky is clear, **then** leave the umbrella at home, **else** it may rain and the umbrella should be taken.

TURN THE PAGE TO REVIEW HOW YOU DID!

How did it go? Was it difficult to get ahead in the game or did you have luck on your side? How many toys did you collect? How about your friend? Are there any strategies for playing a game with conditionals? Why or why not?

HERE'S A TIP!

One example of conditionals is a password. When you want to log into a program, you may need to use a password. If the password is correct, then the computer logs you in, else it sends an error message.

CODING CHALLENGE! _ □ X

Play a game of "Do This!" with some friends. One person is the caller, and calls out "Do this!" They then carry out a specific action, such as hissing like a snake. As long as the caller always starts with the words "Do this," the other players must copy the action. However, if the caller does not say anything before doing an action, and someone copies the action, that player is OUT! The last player left in the game is the winner!

PICTURE PERFECT ___ □ X

Sequencing is the key to creating code that follows a specific order. If the sequence of steps in an algorithm is out of order, a computer program will not work properly. Instructions must be carried out one after the other in the sequence. That is because a computer is designed to follow one command at a time until a task is completed.

In this activity, you will practice following each command, or step, in sequence until you have completed a picture of a toucan.

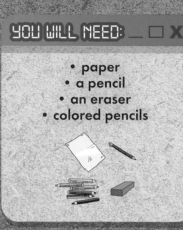

LET'S GET SEQUENCING!

1

Draw the head.

2

Add a wing.

3 Add the body.

4 Add the tail.

5 Add the feet.

6 Add the eye.

7 Add the patch on the chest.

8 Add the beak.

TURN THE PAGE TO SEE HOW YOU DID!

DID YOU KNOW?

Sequences are the building blocks of coding! No coding would be possible without sequencing.

19

How did your picture turn out? Did it look like the toucan below? Did you find it easy to follow the steps in sequence? Did you need to go back, erase, and correct anything? Add on to your picture! You can color in your toucan, add a background, or give the toucan a friend!

Think about something you do every day. It could be getting ready for school in the morning or going to bed at night. What sequence do you follow? If the steps were out of order, would the result be the same?

CODING CHALLENGE! _ □ X

Try creating your own sequence. Use a completed picture of your choice, and then work backward to break it down into the steps required to draw it. Record the steps on a piece of paper, and then give it to a friend to try out. You could also try making up a dance sequence. Play your favorite song and listen for the patterns in the music. Then, come up with a few different moves to go with the music, and perform them in sequence. Try teaching your dance algorithm to a friend!

I HOPE YOU ENJOYED UNPLUGGED CODING!

GLOSSARY _ □ X

algorithm—a step-by-step method to solve a problem

analyze—to look carefully at something to understand how it works and its important parts

bugs—coding errors in a program

code—instructions for a computer

commands—specific instructions to complete a task

communicate—to share knowledge or information

conditionals—lines of programming language that allow different actions depending on true or false information; conditionals are often written in IF/THEN statements.

debugging—finding and removing mistakes in code

output—an action that is a result of a computer program

rain forest—related to a thick, green forest that receives a lot of rain

sequence—a set of instructions that happen in a certain order

TO LEARN MORE

_ □ X

AT THE LIBRARY

Cleary, Brian P. *Bugs That Make Your Computer Crawl: What Are Computer Bugs?* Minneapolis, Minn.: Millbrook Press, 2019.

McCue, Camille. *Getting Started with Coding: Get Creative with Code!* Indianapolis, Ind.: John Wiley and Sons, 2019.

Prottsman, Kiki. *How to Be a Coder.* New York, N.Y.: DK Publishing, 2019.

ON THE WEB

FACTSURFER

Factsurfer.com gives you a safe, fun way to find more information.

1. Go to www.factsurfer.com.

2. Enter "coding with rain forest animals" into the search box and click 🔍.

3. Select your book cover to see a list of related content.

INDEX